PROFITS
In
LAWN CARE

A $100K Business
For A $200 Investment

Author: Roger Krans

Table of contents

Introduction

In the upcoming chapters you will hear about a man who wanted to own a business and retire from his 10 year big box career. This is a true story of persistence, prayer, and a huge desire for independence and freedom. The order of events that took place are duplicatable and can be scaled to just about anyone's situation. Told from the perspective of a first hand observer and friend. We hope you enjoy "Profits in Lawn Care".

Dedication

To anyone who is tired of working for the man and desires much more in life, like having a business of your own.

Chapter 1

The Call for something better

Imagine getting up each day for work knowing that there is something better

out there, but you are tied down to the life you've made for yourself and as you reflect on it, you realize that you were not the only one making those ties. No one knows how it happens, it just does. We want to make all the right decisions and in the process anything with risk gets placed on the back burner. It almost seems inevitable that the more responsibilities we take on, the more our life light gets snuffed out. Risk and chance aren't even in our vocabulary anymore. We can't afford to take a risk because we might lose everything we have worked for. Sound familiar?

This was the case of my friend Charlie. He had a great job, three beautiful children and a textbook wife. Everything seemed great on the outside. However, Charlie had shared with me on several occasions that although he realized how blessed he was to have this kind of lifestyle, he felt that something was missing on the inside. Like there was a call for something bigger and better for him. "There has to be more to this life than just going to work each day, getting a paycheck, and doing it all over again next week " he said. "I want to create something"," I want to challenge myself to see what I'm capable of." I reminded Charlie that those kinds of desires are perfectly natural since we are created in the creator's image. Then I asked him,"If you had the chance to create something and challenge yourself, what would you do?"

I could tell by his change in countenance that I had asked the right question. With a smile I hadn't seen in a long time, he confided in me a plan he had been executing in his mind for some time.

Charlie knew that whatever he had up his sleeve would have to sustain the lifestyle his family had been used to, or his wife would never be onboard. He and I were both firm believers that necessity will push a man to greatness, and it was this principle that gave Charlie the motivation to embark on his new adventure.

CHAPTER 2

A Leap of Faith

Charlie had been a manager in a big box retail store for the last 10 years and

took home a decent salary. He understood that he couldn't just leave that security at the drop of a hat.

But he knew that if he was ever going to make a move it would have to start somewhere.

So on his next day off, Charlie decided to take action, he went to a pawn shop and bought a blower and a rake. A mere $200 investment. His intention was to buy what tools he needed, a few at a time, until he had everything he needed to start his own Lawn Care Business. Now, life has a funny way of blessing you when you step out in faith. And it happened that way for Charlie, because on the way home he started noticing there were several houses in his neighborhood that had large amounts of leaves and pine straw on their roofs. He thought to himself, this is their problem, and I can be their solution. All of a sudden Charlie felt something inside him that he hadn't felt in a long time. He noticed that he was smiling and his mind was racing with ideas. Charlie started writing down the addresses of these homes with the idea that he would send each of them a proposal letter that offered his services to clean off their roofs and gutters for $99.00. "This way I don't have to wait until I get all of my equipment" he thought. "I can start my new business right away. So he sent out the letters and in a few days

Charlie received several requests and so on his next day off he loaded up his ladder, blower, and rake, and headed out to clean off 5 roofs. He was surprised at how easy it was to blow out the gutters and clean off the roof. Charlie made over $500.00 (adding in tips) that first day. He then purchased a hedge trimmer and added hedge trimming to his mail outs along with proposals for full service Lawn Care. It wasn't long before Charlie had a trailer and business cards and started getting repeat clients. Charlie couldn't wait for his days off from the big box store to be able to do what he was most passionate about. Work for himself.

CHAPTER 3

Hit the Ground Running

By now, Charlie's Lawn Care income was making him in 4 days what it took

to make in 2 weeks at his retail job. So Charlie turned in his notice and in a matter of a few weeks, he had enough business to keep him busy 5 days a week. His plan was coming together.

Charlie was ready to expand his business, so he bought a second trailer, outfitted it with all new equipment, and sub -contracted a full time helper. His game plan was to continue to take on new accounts and when they had enough to fill up a route , each sub-contractor would take a trailer and then have two full units on the road. This worked well until Charlie started getting so many new accounts they couldn't keep up. So Charlie hired another subcontractor and bought a third unit.

Now the business grew to the point of Charlie's phone ringing all the time and having to work his days off. So, He hired another sub and assigned him to run his unit. Now that Charlie no longer had a unit to run, he was able to look at his business in a whole new way. He knew there was always room for improvement, so Charlie started implementing new ideas to increase productivity and bring in even more revenue.

When Charlie had purchased his mowers, he made the decision to buy the kind that collect the grass clippings because they leave a nice manicured look to the lawns. The grass clippings are collected all day and dumped in a pile back at the shop. Charlie was coming up on the end of his first year in business and he noticed that the continuous accumulation of grass clippings started to compost into nice black mulch. Several of his customers had asked him throughout the year if he offered topdressing services for their lawns and he always turned them down. But now Charlie saw an opportunity to solve another problem and make his customers happy. So he bought a topdressing machine. It's important to know that topdressing is simply the act of spreading high nutrient compost evenly over lawns to achieve a 3 inch moisture barrier to keep the lawns healthy and retain moisture. This was a huge profitable move for Charlie, taking the very same grass he cuts off his clients lawns, composting it, then selling it back to them as topdressing material. You have to love it when a plan comes together.

Chapter 4

The profits of upselling

I can remember a certain occasion when I was running an errand with Charlie

and he asked if we could stop at his post office box to get his mail (this was his business p.o. box), I said "sure" and we stopped. I walked in with him and I remember how shocked I was when he opened his P.O. box and payment envelops started falling out onto the floor. His box was stuffed full with payments from his clients. I made the comment "maybe you ought to pick up your mail more frequently Charlie", He told me he was just here yesterday. Needless to say, his business was doing so well that he never did have a regret for stepping out in faith. His wife was now involved in the business as well as one of his daughters, and each unit now had two men running them. Charlie couldn't be happier. In about a year and a half he now had three full units of Lawn Maintenance, One special project unit, and one topdressing unit. Business was good.

But Charlie was ready to expand again. It seemed to me that he had not lost one ounce of drive to build something great. So he took some classes at the local community college to learn about soil composition and got his state license to spray herbicides and apply chemicals to the lawns.

Charlie learned about every kind of grass and every plant species. This extra knowledge put him in front of much bigger decision makers and he was able to obtain larger commercial accounts. I would like to mention that I was proud of Charlie. His business grew very quickly, his revenue was impressive, and he became a heavy hitter in the industry. And at no time did any of this success go to his head. He stayed humble and caring for the people he worked with. This was refreshing to see and a great example of Thankfulness.

Chapter 5

Too much business

Through the massive expansion in such a short time, Charlie never lost sight of how blessed he was. He was able to supply several of his subs with their own trailers and let those who wanted to have their own businesses provide for their families (I even saw him give away some of his accounts to start them off).

But Charlie still had that drive within him and it wasn't long before one of the largest Real Estate Companies in town approached him with a proposal to supply Lawn Maintenance for all of their rentals (965 properties to be exact). Charlie jumped at the chance to make such an impact in his business. I have to say that it was a lot to bite off at one time, and Charlie and his teams kept up with it as long as they could. But they eventually burned out and couldn't find enough new subs quick enough. It was a lesson well learned. Charlie's revenue was well over the six figure threshold at this time and he and his subs were well compensated. Between the commercial accounts and the Real Estate Companies, Charlie decided a change would have to be made, so he stopped taking on residential accounts and started referring them to his old proteges.

Chapter 6

New Horizons

Once the business started getting back to where it was scalable again, Charlie decided to break into new areas of service. He launched a side business called "Gravetenders". This was a new unit he put on the road for the sole purpose of maintaining gravesites. This proved to be a very profitable endeavor. Very low overhead, and the two man unit could service 20 graves per day at $50.00 each.

Charlie also branched out into the pressure washing realm. This was also profitable, but came with many headaches. Turns out a pressure washer can damage many surfaces if it's placed in the wrong hands. This side of the business did not last long.

One of the perks of having commercial accounts is that they are constantly wanting to update their landscaping. So whenever they would request removing plants and replacing them with something different, Charlie would challenge his crews to sell the old plants to one of the other accounts. This was very profitable because the plants were free.

This gave Charlie the idea to start a plant nursery. Now the great thing about plants is that you can propagate them and have an endless supply to sell. This proved to be very profitable in itself, but also for Charlie's Lawn Business and once word got out, other landscape companies started buying from them as well.

With Charlie's businesses being in Florida, they could operate year round without having to worry about snow and weather (except for an occasional hurricane), which brings us to another very profitable portion of the business.

Storm Clean-up. This is worth mentioning because after a bad storm it was not uncommon for the clean-up crews to make as much in a month as the business made in a year.

Especially when you have a place to burn or dispose of storm debris. Fallen trees can be cut into lengths and sold to lumber companies. So they got paid to remove the fallen trees and then to sell the logs to the sawmills. This was an example of getting something out of nothing. Very profitable..

Another venture Charlie recognized as an income producing opportunity was Palm Tree Trimming. He had a crew that he sub-contracted out to do nothing but trim palm trees for $25.00 each. They averaged 80 per day (aprox $2,000 per day)

One day Charlie received a call from his wife who told him that their pine straw supplier was going up on their prices again. This concerned Charlie as it was the third increase that year. So he made a few calls and found out where he could get a couple of pine straw balers. These are machines that you feed pine straw into and it molds and ties the pine straw into an easy to handle bale. Charlie made the trip to Alabama to purchase them and on the way home he contemplated where he could get large amounts of pine straw. Most pine straw farms will charge you by the bale to rake it up, clean it and bale it. So Charlie came up with a brilliant idea. He drove to the nearest State Park and asked the park rangers if he could clean up the grounds for them. They jumped at the chance to have it done for them. So the next day Charlie brought a crew with him and 3 large trailers and they took backpack blowers (the rangers use rakes) and blew all the pine straw into huge piles and rolled them onto the trailers. This was a win for both Charlie and the rangers. They got their park cleaned and Charlie got free pine straw for his balers. He implemented this process in many of the surrounding State Parks. This is the kind of mindset each entrepreneur needs to have. Thinking beyond the normal walls. Letting necessity push you into finding better (more profitable) ways to accomplish the desired goals.

Chapter 7

Circumventing the system

Disclaimer: It should NOT be implied that the author agrees, promotes, or expresses that the following information is right, wrong, legal or illegal. The information is simply being shared with the reader that this is the way Charlie ran his business.

Charlie never wanted to expand his business in the typical way that most people do. His wife was his administrator and he was a sole proprietor. When Charlie started getting more business than he could handle, he didn't want to become a slave to the idea of having employees and having to pay for their insurance and labor costs, so Charlie would sub-contract his accounts to other sole proprietors who carried their own insurance. He would have them sign a "Hold Harmless" agreement and a contract describing the scope of the work and the day of week it was to be executed. Contracts were renewed yearly and sub-contractors were paid weekly. If the subs worked an entire year with no major issues, Charlie would give them a generous bonus.

This system worked well as long as I can remember for Charlie. If there was ever an easier way to do something, Charlie was going to find it. I'm reminded of another instance where this came into play. In the early days when Charlie had exceeded 20 accounts, his wife suggested that he look into an accounting program to help with the billing and to keep up to date records. Charlie agreed with her that they needed one and so he researched several companies until he found one that would work well for them.

At first, this company was helpful and supportive in training Charlie and his wife on all the ins and outs of the bookkeeping process. But once Charlie committed to their program, the company increased their costs on the services and the materials (billing supplies, software updates, ect…). So once again, Charlie was at the mercy of the company and very upset and discouraged. So after much contemplation, Charlie decided to take the billing materials to a print shop to see if they could be reproduced. He found one that would work with him and no longer had to pay the increased prices of the money hungry accounting firm. As a matter of fact, Charlie also found a software programer that put together a tailored program for his wife, so they were able to cut the ties altogether with the accounting firm. As you can probably tell by now, Charlie never was the kind of person who would sit still while someone would try to take advantage of him. I watched him on many occasions helping others (even strangers) who were being taken advantage of. To this day Charlie is a firm believer in "you reap what you sow".

Conclusion: Call to action

I hope you've found Charlie's story to be one of inspiration and a glimpse into the world of Lawn Care and small business start-up. I believe anyone who wants to start their own Lawn Care business, or even if you already have a small Lawn Care Company, would benefit from some of the plans and procedures that have been shared in his story. One of the most unique things about Charlie's adventure is the fact that he started it with only a $200 investment and turned it into a 6 figure business in just 18 months.

Now Charlie couldn't have accomplished this without hard work, dedication, and a drive to make a positive change in his life. Sometimes the pain of wanting a better life has to become greater than the pain of change. And it all starts with you having enough drive to stop what you are doing right now, get up, and make the first move toward your better life. It has to start somewhere. We are all fearfully and wonderfully made. There is more inside of you than you realize. We are not created to survive, we are created to thrive. I overheard Charlie one morning telling his crews before they headed out for the day a very inspiring lesson. He said" When you pull up to an account, stop for just a moment and take a close look at it. Walk around the property and ask yourself, "If we charge $200 each time we service this account, what can we do to make it $300?" Can we ask if they want their hedges trimmed? Can we ask if we can fertilize the grounds? Can we ask if we can spray the beds? Can we ask if we can blow the roof?" "What can we do to turn our $200 into $300 today?" If we do this at each account, each day, how much more revenue can we generate?"

 I shared this last truth about Charlie because this is the mindset of a great entrepreneur. Maybe you have that same drive in you.

Now get off your tail and use the gifts that God has given you.

We are only given so much time in this life. Go make something great happen!!!

I would be incredibly thankful if you took 2 minutes to submit a review of the things you liked about this book on whatever platform you purchased it from. Thank you in advance. May God bless you richly !

The following short stories are excerpts from Charlie's many mishaps in the Lawn Care industry. We added these happenings with the idea that perhaps if you read about them, they might not happen to you. Some of them will seem hard to believe, but know this, anything is possible with God.

The first one that comes to mind happened in Charlie's first few months after getting started. Charlie had just received a phone call that his new mower was in. He couldn't wait to go pick it up and start using it. This mower was, at the time, top of the line for residential accounts. It retailed just over $14,000 and was in our humble opinion the best mower on the market. It was an American made beauty that was manufactured by a family that had been in the business for many years (there is still a diecast model of it that sits on my desk as this is being written). Charlie had shelled out some big bucks for it and had it loaded up and ready for the next days cutting. He wanted to break it in on his biggest and best account that was located in the ritzy section of town and owned by a doctor. The property was huge and the back yard had three sections that were terraced down to the ocean. Charlie had used zero turn mowers in the past and was quite proficient with them. Although this was also a zero turn mower, it was a little bit different, as most zero turns have two small wheels in front and two larger wheels in back, this new mower had the two small wheels in front, the two larger wheels in the middle and a fifth wheel in the back which made it able to turn much more sharply (Charlie was NOT used to this). Everything was going well to begin with and Charlie was getting the hang of this mower quickly, that is, until he got too close to the edge of the first landscaping tier. As the back wheel tried to turn the mower around, it got caught on one of the landscaping blocks that held up the 8 foot terrace wall and the mower (and Charlie) started to slide off backwards. There really wasn't any time to think, Charlie felt the mower sliding backwards and heard the wall start to crumble. All he had time to do was pray a two word prayer "LORD JESUS", and then THUD! The impact was devastating. As Charlie regained his senses his first thought was "Can I move my toes? Can I move my fingers" Am I hurt?" Charlie was still sitting in the mower seat facing towards the sky. The back end of the mower was imbedded in the ground. It was still running and the oil was pouring out onto the hot muffler which was making billowing clouds of smoke surrounding the grounds and neighbors yards. Charlie jumped off and shut everything down. Performed a quick assessment of himself (bruised leg, sore back and annihilated ego). And just stood there looking at his brand new $14K mower. Dollar signs were starting to make their way into his mind as he wondered what this was going to cost in repairs. After all, he just drove his new mower off an 8ft terrace (backwards) and embedded it into the ground. Charlie sat down for a few moments to collect his thoughts and to let the mower cool off a bit. The great thing about Charlie, he was never one to dwell on negative things. So he jumped up and with all that he had left within him, he pushed the mower over and started to clean it off and look for damages. The more he cleaned the more he couldn't believe his eyes. Charlie couldn't find anything wrong with the mower. He looked it over and over again as if he was lying to himself. He just could not find any damage. With a deep breath he turned the key and it fired right up. It started smoking but Charlie just figured the spilled oil would have to burn off. And he was right, after a few minutes, he sat back down and finished mowing. As the days went by and Charlie had time to reflect on what had happened, he realized that there were so many ways that could have gone. So many ways it could have turned out tragic. Rest assured, to this day, Charlie spends many waking hours thanking God and sharing this story with whoever shows interest. Just another testimony of the importance of praying protection around yourself each and every day.

This next story happened right after the "Can my mower fly backwards?" incident you just read about. A huge development company bought a large tract of land out by the beach and had just finished building the infrastructure and was starting to sell new build homes and Charlie received a call from one of the new home owners to come out and give an estimate for year round lawn care. As Charlie pulled up to the home he noticed how well it was landscaped but there were small white balls everywhere around the house. As he got out of his truck he knew right away what they were by the smell, "Moth balls". The client came out to greet him and after the initial business was complete, Charlie asked him about the moth balls. The client told Charlie that he had read that snakes don't like moth balls and so my wife and I are protecting our home from snakes. Charlie thanked the man and went on his way. The man ended up hiring Charlie and as several weeks went by, each time Charlie would service the account, he and the client would have discussions about snakes and the moth balls. Then one rainy day when Charlie had a little "down time", he decided to research Florida snakes and the idea of moth balls repelling them. Charlie educated himself and was all prepared to engage the client the next time he serviced the account. When that day came, Charlie pulled up like he always did and waited for the man to come out and have their ten minute discussion. The man never showed so Charlie serviced the account and when he got back in his truck he had a message from the client that stated they had travelled back to their other home in South Florida because they encountered a rattlesnake in their yard and it scarred them so bad that they didn't want to come back here until cooler weather. They also left instructions for Charlie to purchase 3 cases of moth balls and spread them out around the house. Now Charlie was not one to question assignments, however, after the research he did, it seemed silly to apply even more moth balls than the property already had. Especially when Charlie learned that moth balls DO NOT repel snakes. You see, snakes smell with their tongues, so practices like using moth balls (odors) are not to be relied upon.

So being a good steward, Charlie didn't want the clients to waste their money on a practice that was most likely not going to work. So Charlie gave them a call and when he shared what he had learned the client became furious. He told Charlie that he had gotten the information about the moth balls from a very reliable source and he didn't appreciate Charlie second guessing him.
So, Charlie bought the 3 cases of moth balls and evenly distributed them around the house and landscaping. Needless to say, it looked like a hail storm had just occurred. There were so many moth balls around this property it looked ridiculous. Well Charlie knew that Summer was almost over and the last of the Summer rains would eventually melt the moth balls away. So Charlie continued to service the account while the clients were away and laughed every time he pulled up to the home, except this time. Because while he was walking around the house inspecting what needed to be done, there, at the base of a pine tree, was a huge rattlesnake, all coiled up, just

sitting there, and I'll give you one guess what was sitting in the middle of the coil? That's right, 3 moth balls. The snake had coiled himself around three moth balls and was as content as can be. Charlie told his helper to go get a bucket and a grabber, and while he waited, Charlie took several pictures of the snake with the moth balls in the middle. They removed the snake and relocated it and when they left, Charlie drove straight to the nearest photo store and got the pictures on his phone developed into 8x10 portraits. He placed them in an envelope and sent them first class to his client. He texted the client and told him to watch for a surprise in the mail. The next day Charlie received an apology from his client.

Bonus Chapter 2

To this day, Charlie and I still get together and reminisce about many of his adventures in Lawn Care. He taught me many things about nature and the signs that God gives to let you know important changes are coming, for instance, He knows that the first sign of Spring (At least in North Florida) is when he sees the Carpenter Bees start to fly around. This sign acknowledges that the hot weather is only two-three weeks away. Another is when the wasps are super aggressive when the queen is just coming out of hibernation (most wasps die off when the cold weather comes and the queen finds a warm place to hibernate). These are just a few of the signs my friend Charlie taught me about. They are interesting to know because now I look for them each year. Another sign of spring is when the Kites start to show up. They fly to South America in the fall and come back to Florida in the spring. It never ceases to amaze me how they know just when the right time is.

It's the same thing in the fall. The signs that tell the cold weather is on the way. The spiders spend most of the summer in trees and on the ground feeding, but when winter is about three weeks out, the spiders all start building webs as an aid to catch more food to prepare themselves for diapause (the state where their bodies slow down and go dormant for winter). This is also the time when wasps get aggressive again just before the cold weather comes. It's a great time for fishermen too. They know what species run during this time of year. God has always given us signs to tell when its time to prepare. For the purpose of this book we will share a story that Charlie got to see all too often in the business. This happened just about every year to the new guys that came into the business the Spring or Summer before their first winter. As the weather gets colder the grass will go dormant at some point. This does not mean the grass stops growing, it just slows down significantly. The problem is, when this happens, the grass also turns a darker shade of brown. This tends to be a problem for the lazy landscaper because he has not educated himself in the finer points of Lawncare. So, one or two things happen. Either the client complains that their grass looks dead or the uneducated landscaper panics and thinks their clients lawn has died. Either way, the newbie runs to his nearest landscape supply store and buys a bunch of Nitrogen to apply on the lawn. Now it's important to understand that Nitrogen is one of the three important macronutrients that are found in most of the fertilizers on the market. Nitrogen pushes the production of chlorophyll in the grass which gives it that stunning green color. The problem with applying it in the winter, is that it will bring the grass out of its dormant stage and give it a huge boost of growth. This becomes a real issue when a frost comes and freezes this new growth. In essence, it can kill the entire lawn. Charlie saw many newbies that had to resod their clients' lawns at their expense. Bottom line, make sure you educate yourself in the ways of natural lawn progression.

This next story comes to you only by the Grace of God. If things had gone a different way, I'm not sure I could have told it. The story starts with a new helper Charlie had brought on by helping out a friend. It was one of those "can you please give my son a job?" deals. Charlie knew better, but most of the time his heart was bigger than his brain. So he contracted him to help out. Now Charlie's business was growing rapidly and he had just landed several of the local school grounds. It was convenient to service the schools on the weekends when there was no one around. So Charlie and his helper went to the first school and Charlie gave him detailed training on what he wanted him to do. Charlie was used to servicing the schools by himself but since he had this helper, he decided to give him the easiest job he had. Trim the hedges. All this guy had to do was trim up the hedges and blow the trimmings out into the grass where the mower could bag them up. Now Charlie kept a pretty close eye on his new helper. Every time he would mow near him, he would inspect the hedges and see if he needed any help. All was looking good. Now the reason I'm telling this particular story is not so much because of WHAT happened, it's because of what COULD have happened. As Charlie came around the corner he noticed his helper climbing inside the hedges, frantically moving around like something was wrong. Charlie stopped mowing and went over to see what was going on. Just then he saw, clenched in his helpers hand a cut CCTV cable. While cutting the hedges, he had cut through the school's Closed Circuit Television Cable. This was not good. Charlie could feel his blood pressure starting to climb. But that wasn't the worst of it, when Charlie questioned him about it, the helper said "This isn't the only one". He had cut through 4 CCTV cables in the first couple of hours on the job. Now this was on a Saturday and Charlie didn't know if he could get someone to come out and fix it by Monday when classes started. He called around to every place he could think of but they were all closed. Charlie didn't want to lose his good reputation with the school board. So he thought and thought, and then an idea came to him. One of the men on another crew used to install cable TV. Perhaps he would be able to help. So Charlie called him and he drove right over. Had all the tools he needed in his truck, and fixed the cables. Crisis averted.

Charlie was not happy with his new helper, but now they were behind and needed to finish the school. So he told the helper to put up the hedge trimmer, grab the blower, and just go behind the mower and blow off the sidewalks. "He can't mess this up" Charlie thought. As Charlie finished mowing, he looked behind him and his helper was nowhere in sight. Charlie started looking for him and when he found him he saw that the blower had run out of gas and the helper was filling it up with the gas can. So Charlie told him to finish up blowing and they would be done for the day. Charlie drove the mower up onto the trailer as the helper put away the blower and they headed down the road. As Charlie pulled out into traffic he merged with the other drivers and as he looked in his side mirror, he saw his $500 hedge trimmer go sailing off the trailer. Charlie couldn't stop because of the traffic and as he kept driving he saw a man in a motorhome stop and pick up the hedge trimmer and drive off. Charlie asked very sternly "I guess you didn't put the hedge trimmer where it belongs?" The helper simply said "sorry", and went back to looking at his phone. No remorse, no conviction, not even an ounce of care. When they got back to the warehouse, Charlie paid him for the hours he worked and told him he was done. The guy took the money and left. Now unfortunately it doesn't end here.

Charlie got up early Monday morning to run by the school to make sure it looked presentable before the teachers started showing up. As he walked the school grounds he came up to the kindergarten area where they play outside and there, sitting on the monkey bars, was the gas can, full of gas, that dingdong had left when he filled up the blower. "THANK GOD" Charlie exclaimed, as he grabbed it and left.

So once again, can you imagine what could have happened if the children had come out to play and the gas can fell on them or splashed gas on them? One thing Charlie always taught and followed himself, "Before you start your day, take time out to pray!". This was a staple in Charlie's life and one of the things I most admired about the man. So, to close this chapter, there are two takeaways from this story. **Number one**, on every trailer, EVERYTHING should have a home. Every tool, every accessory, everything. This way it is easy to glance at the trailer and see if anything is missing or not in it's home. **Number two**, Never start your day, until you take time to pray. God Bless !